ALLISON

ALSO BY MARISA SILVA-DUNBAR

#becky

When Goddesses Wake

Allison

QUERENCIA

Querencia Press, LLC
Chicago Illinois

QUERENCIA PRESS

© Copyright 2022
Marisa Silva-Dunbar.

LIBRARY OF CONGRESS CATALOGNG-IN-PUBLICATION DATA

ISBN 978 1 80016 291 4

www.querenciapress.com

First Published in 2022

Querencia Press, LLC
Chicago IL

Printed & Bound in the United States of America

"The fact is that we have no way of knowing if the person who we think we are is at the core of our being. Are you a decent girl with the potential to someday become an evil monster, or are you an evil monster that thinks it's a decent girl?"

"Wouldn't I know which one I was?"

"Good God, no. The lies we tell other people are nothing to the lies we tell ourselves."

—Derek Landy, Death Bringer

TABLE OF CONTENTS

Pro·em[1]

"Character is shy yet codependent, searching for love in all the wrong men. Character confides in others at her own risk. Character is fatigued and hollow, suffers from self-doubt, a sense of worthlessness…A woman fights to save her soul…Requires an actress that will leave an audience speechless."

—*Amber Tamblyn, "Untitled Actress"*

---

[1] Definition of proem
1 preliminary comment, preface
2 prelude

Expecting adoration: April 1, 2018
Erasure poem from <u>Frank Report</u>'s article on Allison Mack

Allison was a cornucopia of ramblings—
devotions from Mexico,
a forced role in the scheme—women.
Branded, she has been the criminal.

She writes about mental confusion:
"My mentor:
consumed with a lesson
inside of my skull.
~~*he*~~ *taught me to take more   deeply*
the better I remembered.
That voice in my head now irrelevant."

The slave branded, preyed on,
        sleep-deprived and malnourished—
gave of herself, destroyed her life—
she is a human tragedy—
trapped, ignored, in decline.

Elements of you

Coffee beans spilled on the white tiled countertop
next to the blue mason jar of daisies and azaleas;
a map with silver push-pins of where you've been—
blue where you hoped your feet would carry you.

Photos of the dusty ghost towns on Route 66,
abandoned gas stations and train tracks,
blue skies dotted with coral clouds like carnation
buds, your pictures of the cello player
at Liverpool St. Station; concert and theater tickets
tucked into the corners of your mirror,
a love letter from your former fiancé folded
between the pages of "The Prophet."
And there were always pictures of *your* bridge,
from every angle and season. You wanted
to make it clear these were elements of you.

They are echoes from lifetimes you let slip
from the palms of your hands.
I don't know where they went;
maybe they're the secret kept under your pillow,
maybe these moments are when you started to fade.

Body Stuff

It knows what it really wants to reject,
despite coercion and manipulation.
It would purge the experience like
bitter, slimy bile you retch in the mornings.

It's not confused in its response—
the nausea, the dazed state it stumbles
around in afterwards—the ground
never really seems solid anymore.

~~his~~ "energy" is an assault;
did some part of you know
when it happened to you too?

Genesis

"Now the serpent was more crafty than any of the wild animals the LORD God had made. He said to the woman, "Did God really say, 'You must not eat from any tree in the garden'?"

—Genesis 3:1

The Introduction: November 14, 2006

We are now witnesses to the origin
—here is where ~~he~~ ensnares you.

You are mesmerized—girlish—giggly,
and desperate for your worth to be seen
by this ~~man~~ in a sweatband and kneepads.
We know it's just a seedy façade. Some
of us have at one point, wanted to be
loved by a mediocre ~~man~~.

~~he~~ already sees you as prey—
already wants to break you into bite-
sized pieces. You crumble so easily,
gulping sobs as ~~he~~ destroys your joy,
calls it artificial. ~~he~~ wants you to
become reliant on ~~him~~ to find true
exultation.

You dissolve.

the deceiver

Many will say they didn't see rippling,
scarlet flags surrounding ~~him~~ —or they learned
to quell the thick bile churning in their stomachs,
a warning to run away from ~~his~~ grasp.
Still, a few follow ~~him~~ into the abyss.

Those who fled acknowledge ~~his~~ skills as a salesman—
a Lange Wapper shapeshifting, performing magic tricks,
making you think you are the only one to witness
the show. Listen as ~~he~~ speaks in riddles, conning
you into thinking ~~he~~ holds the answers.
Let ~~him~~ lure you into waters for a false baptism;
~~he'll~~ drown you then feast on your blood.

December 2nd, 2011: Warrior Heart and Buddha Soul
Remixed poem from Allison Mack's Blog

I.

I have burned
through hell alone.
Felt crazy—like spinning in circles
struggling to catch ground before
I strike the earth—a lightning bolt.

II.

My mother abandoned me in a stale state; decay crept
through my childhood home with quiet potency.

I woke up—pulled my damp body down the hall
trying to outrun the poison.

III.

Last summer I made a plan—
I invited two friends over for breakfast.
We chatted over a sumptuous feast
of sun-dried tomato strata, fruit salad
drizzled with honey and lime zest.
We giggled as we sipped sweet, milky chai.
Even Edith Piaf welcomed my explosion of life.

December 16th, 2011: 7 Stages
Remixed poem from Allison Mack's Blog

1. SHOCK & DENIAL
I do not feel well.

2. PAIN & GUILT
overwhelm me—
I can barely breathe.

My body is a hellscape.

3. ANGER & BARGAINING
burning—I am not willing to accept
that I am a human being with limitations.
I do what I have always done: punish myself until I submit.

Then comes the bargaining.

4. "DEPRESSION", REFLECTION, LONELINESS
My flesh froths, blisters.
I sit in my dark room—a little lost girl.

I've rejected myself—
my body, my enemy.
It's a woman's body—betraying my desires.

My body rebels against me, the oppressor.

5. THE UPWARD TURN
I go outside. I feel the air on my skin
and the warmth of the sun.
I give my abused body a bath—I soak my sores.

I am coming back to life.

6. RECONSTRUCTION & WORKING THROUGH
At night, I decide everything will change:
I throw away women—size negative zero,
crystallized dreams.

Yes, everything will change.

7. ACCEPTANCE & HOPE
My body, always offering more has carried me:
through China's foothills, made room for wine and cheese.

Maybe now I can work with her.

December 24th, 2011: Gift of Presence
Remixed poem from Allison Mack's Blog

It's Christmas NYC, I race across my bridge
into the madness of holiday jingles and frenetic shoppers
scouring the streets for that perfect present.
Colored lights adorn street lamps—my city is all aglow.

I'm nestled in my favorite gift—a multi-colored,
hand-knit scarf soaked with the smell of gardenia
and jasmine oils—enchanted with my friend's love
and healing. I am not ashamed to wear
the patched holes representing my scars.

My friend knitted this bountiful comforter in
the back of theatres, on park benches, in the corners
of bookstores on Sunday afternoons as the light faded
from the sky; in cafes sipping on hot chocolate,
on the velvet couch near her fireplace.

As she wrapped the stitches through her fingers
she entwined our memories: meandering through the plaza
of a sleepy Spanish town; late night phone calls
while snowed in the city—warming me as sleep
slipped into the room. The time we had a vegan feast
of potato malai kofta and coconut chai.

My dear friend knows I prefer to wear the mask
of independence—perfectly constructed, and painted
with precision. No cracks can show through.
She can feel underneath *I am dying for a hug.*
She created one for me to wear
unraveled from her heart.

As an old friend of Allison's: She needs help ASAP, August 29th, 2017

Remixed poem from <u>Frank Report</u>

She needs to hold some responsibility,
(like hot stones tied to her hands),

But I come to her defense, a little.
She's been coming apart,
her mind—fragile since the beginning.

~~he~~'s enjoyed   twisting her
~~he~~ and ~~his~~ women have delighted
in screwing with   her brain,
she continues to serve,
to procure young women
~~he~~ can abuse.

On the nights   she cries and begs
for forgiveness,   ~~he~~ applauds.

January 3rd, 2012: The Cynical Romantic
Remixed poem from Allison Mack's Website

I've had two major loves,
both with the promise of forever.
I tattooed one's name just below
my collarbone (a permanent brand).
With the other, I adopted a menagerie—
they remained after it ended.

Our love wasn't splattered
in the technicolor of a John Hughes film.
The yearning for a connection
as deep as the Marianas trench—
something tethering me to the Earth—
flows through me like a calming
lazy river, making me full.

February 28, 2012: Full Stop
Remixed poem from Allison Mack's Website

A simple afternoon:
Maple syrup slowly flowing down
a stack of fluffy-warm pancakes,
The Brooklyn Bridge, between two archways—
you can see past Ellis Island.
My favorite sunset—
hides right behind the Statue of Liberty.

Here is where infinite possibilities live.

March 15th, 2012: What now?
Remixed poem from Allison Mack's Blog

A box of pictures,
of rainy days in Vancouver,
when I was a haunted girl—
no *me* behind the mask.

I want to build the actual me:
a woman that helps all women.
No make-up, necessary.
My life will expand with curiosity:
pushing at corners of the Earth,
collecting stories from the oceans
and continents.

You will find me
in my second spring—
in coffee shops, sitting on a plush, blue couch
writing books, and magazine articles.
I plan to be complete newness—
a baby giraffe standing for the first time.

I just want to listen to crickets serenading at twilight.

May 8th, 2012: Mentors
Remixed poem from Allison Mack's Blog

I.
Take a deeper look—
I am shaped by them:

in the wooden, silver and gold bangles I keep,
in the oversized trousers I store
next to men's dress shirts and vests,
in the silk, Indian scarves that drape over porcelain hooks.

II.
I am committed to a ~~man~~ who has qualities I long for,
but don't yet understand.
I am hypnotized,
free falling into who ~~he~~ thinks I should be.
I am shaped by ~~him~~.

I swing between the woman
I feel unfurling in my belly   and what
~~he~~ *really* wants,   simple and superficial.

III.
(I am diminished,   a woman caught
in a corner web,
trapped.   I gave up empathy for a sense of
belonging,
          how numbing.)
                              Pay attention!

IV.
We are all just seeking mentors in disguise,
offering these moments with quiet potency.

Love-bombed: November 23rd, 2017
Remixed poem from *Frank Report*

Allison was ripe for the picking:
wealthy, at the start of a quarter
life crisis, searching for a cause
where she could take root and bloom—
there was no one to tether her.
Not the paramour she kissed in moonlight,
not even her sweet-sponging mom&dad.

I was there her first weekend.

The ladies love-bombed her
with candied words for wooing.
She indulged it—soaked in their adoration.

The ladies knew how to get their talons
into her bones—how to make her feel
like she was chosen—the high priestess
they'd scoured the globe for.

Before the weekend was over,
they wanted to know, *was she willing to be sacrificed*
to *their* ~~god~~? For the ritual she'd have to swallow
~~his~~ words, lie on their altar and let ~~him~~ carve her
into ~~his~~ ideal, and ~~he~~ would crown her with Venus
trap, bilberry, oleander, and pomegranate blossoms.

She flew out the next day, to meet
the ~~god~~ she'd been waiting for.

March 6th, 2014: My Global Museum Tour, Museum #1: The Barnes Museum
Remixed poem from Allison Mack's Blog

Spend a few lifetimes here:
disappear in cities across the globe,
blend into brightly painted murals and mosaic tiles.

I woke up early—walked along the cobblestone streets—
past old row houses. Leftover morning frost
coated the tall, angular building made of limestone.
I remember the ivy frame, a still reflecting pond.

Through the giant wooden doors,
I heard historians whispering into my ear.
I become the one rhapsodizing with Matisse & Picasso,
discussing tones & textures, lines & color with Modigliani.
I effuse with Van Gogh about his newest, bluest piece.

We sink into one another—I am the collector.

March 14th, 2014: My Global Museum Tour, Museum #2: The Neue Galerie

Remixed poem from Allison Mack's Blog

The Shanghai Bistro:
a typical Vancouver evening
is an impressionist masterpiece:
the street lights reflect off the rain and puddles.
We've become a staple here—
sipping glasses of white wine sharing
the last of the Chinese green beans and guotie.

I have never seen him so tidy.
A true gentleman, he always opens my door,
puts his napkin in his lap.
I call him Big Daddy. He subtly puts me in my place—
the secret is all characters are looking to get laid.

The natural reddening of my cheeks
in his presence has become a reflex.

He teaches me how to be decadent, curious.
He exposes me to the raw, delicious world,
I've been so afraid of exploring. We've dissected
Shakespeare, the elements of a good wine,
how to make wickedly naughty sexual innuendos.
He is my guide to the world of art—
shows me the beauty in all things dirty.
He likes the smell of sweat.

He has gifted me a list of "divine places not to be missed."

In the 60's, Manhattan permeated with bohemians.
I picture John living in his TriBeca loft—
Woodstock 24/7. I wish I was there with him,
bare feet and sunflowers in my hair,

supple sun-kissed shoulders,
and peasant skirts caressing the floor.

There, I embrace the bitter, dirty,
sexy, and sloppy parts of me.

I finally understand why John has been pushing me
to admit when I am horny and unkempt.
He loves the rawness of human beings;

the more he sees me—the more I let go.

Je ne sais quoi
Remixed poem from Allison Mack's Website

I'm attracted to the struggle of women—
I lived my life conflicted,
never satisfied, raging.

I felt threatened by them—
Women:
with painted lips and cat eyes in cashmere sweaters,
the CEOs in crisp, tailored business suits and pumps,
tough chicks in leather pants and white tank tops,
"Good Girls," in white sundresses and heart-shaped glasses,
hikers in a ponytail with a backpack, and toned arms,
the club beauties in tight, bright body
clinging dresses and bling,
Gamer Girls in concert tees and torn jeans.

This was a secret I kept—
I wanted to be able to sink
into the women I surrounded myself with.

An accomplice: November 23rd, 2017
Remixed poem from Frank Report

In the real world, she is evil:
the bad seed in blonde braids—
a she-demon committed to
supplying her ~~god~~ with beautiful (unwilling)
maidens and pussy (hers. theirs.).
She must find followers to sacrifice.
She's already given the ultimate devotion—
~~his~~ initials burned on her hip.

~~he~~ makes her weep,
spins ~~his~~ bile into a sugar sculpture
she eagerly consumes.
                              She thinks this is happiness.

June 25th, 2014: Life & Death
Remixed poem from Allison Mack's Website

She was the first of ~~his~~ lovers I watched perish.

After they shaved her head,
it wasn't long until her body followed.

It's a rapid descent when we are no longer useful.

The last time I saw her,
she gave a speech at a friend's wedding,
ashen 80 pounds of flesh and muscles
Twisted around a skeletal frame.

                        Most of ~~his~~ women
transform into ghastly creatures.

That night we drank champagne,
and danced to The Jackson 5.

                        Celebration is
annihilation.

July 3rd, 2014: Collecting Heroes
Remixed poem from Allison Mack's Blog

I.
I want to be a woman of:
strength,
dignity,
focus,
integrity.

I want to be a woman,
who won't apologize.

II.
I watch my heroes every morning,
while I drink chamomile tea.
I sup their wise words with teaspoons of honey,
slather their stories onto my toast.

They're put together, poised:
the ingénue fluttering her doe eyes,
a screen goddess with stiletto red nails, a dirty martini,
the earth mother with dirt stained skirts—
and millennia in her eyes.

I want to be that type of woman.
They don't apologize.

III.
One of my greatest heroes told me
~~he~~ could mold me into the ideal   woman.
take me home,   and make me ~~his~~
science experiment,   blossoming in ~~his~~ lab.

I want to be ~~his~~ woman;   whatever catastrophe ~~he~~
creates,

~~he~~ won't apologize.

Wonderstruck

There's something not stable about her. And ... she's got this gaggle of
women that she's mentoring that are not doing well. - Mark Vicente

The young ingénue, playing the witty
and pretty best friend to *the* Super.

You're the Pied Piper, these women want
to follow you into the unknown.
They trust you to lead them through fields—
towards a bright sky-blue salvation.

They don't see you grasping at the air
trying to steady yourself, how your own eyes
are wrapped one hundred times with *cellophane*.
They don't know the tune inside your head, leads you
and them to the cliffs—how even if
you all survive the fall, shore and serenity
are more than a day's swim away.

The melody haunts you—you want it
to feel like warm caramel. You want
these women to feast on your wisdom—
worship you like a goddess. Bring you
lotus blossoms, marigolds and roses.

Pretend you are floating instead
of rapidly sinking into quicksand.

July 13, 2014: After a Year
Remixed poem from Allison Mack's Website

I see ~~your~~ name,
my cheeks flush.
It's been over a year and still.

Secretly, I am counting down the mornings,
thinking about that afternoon.
I want to be pretty,
to show off
I've changed.

Honey Pot

I once knew someone like you;
they bragged about being glitter in the sunlight
like it's not shiny micro-plastic
that everyone dreads—
that poisons the earth.

I knew a monster like you;
she thought it was simpler to be
the lure into the game,
the honey that draws
those desperate for a taste.
The one who doesn't know
how to move the pieces on her own.
Always waiting for ~~his~~ whispers,
~~his~~ hands to cover yours.

I knew a husk of woman like you:
who twisted herself into something vile—
a demon in the night, lurking,
even the snakes won't go near.
When her lover left,
she was just a shell waiting
for the next man to fill her.

And yours—
~~he~~'ll trade you for a newer version,
leave you when it comes crashing down.

Ugh, men.

November 5th, 2014: You know those days...
Remixed poem from Allison Mack's Blog

I.

This morning,
I melted.
The pressure of my fears
liquefying me.

II.

The closeness of humans, their desires—
their wills—crush me until all I can do is weep space:
yards of grass,
a city block,
a highway in the desert,
an indigo ocean raging away from land,
miles of stardust.

I disappear.

III.

A constant refrain whispers in the idle hours:
Be anyone but you.
See the cracks in you.
Repair what parts of you that still have a chance.
Rewind to a time before you were broken.

Wake up!

November 10, 2014: Imagine!
Remixed poem from Allison Mack's Website

I used my imagination,
hours in the backyard.
I was a flower fae—
a stick was a magic wand.
I could make everything bloom;
I lived in the garden of eternal summer.

Then there was the turning:
the rigidness of ice cold *perfection*—
legs smooth as polished stones,
makeup a flawless mask,
the routine of manners and sweetness.
I felt like *when the chain on your bike*
breaks and catches the tire.
My attempt to be a "good girl," killed my magic.
I was kindling in a fire, and I incinerated.

Frustrated, I am uncomfortable with constant desire—
I find I cannot open up.

I used to dream.

Cracks

"She needed to really look into herself and fix this—this impulse that she has to destroy another woman."

Mark Vicente on Allison Mack

You joined a group to learn how to be friends with women.
Were you deficient in this ability your whole life?
Did you go around hanging with the boys,
telling them you're not like other girls?

Tell me you confessed your jealousy was rotting you
from the inside out, or that you couldn't contain it—
it was constantly spilling from you,
that it was obvious for years.

~~he~~ knew how to twist this into your cruelty,
make you an eager accomplice. You have power
over your fears—other women. You think you earn
~~his~~ love this way, that you won't be discarded like
the others. By then it won't be just your mind
~~he~~ poisons; watch how you truly fester and wither.

Here is the secret: ~~he~~ is content draining you.
You are just a meal to be consumed,
and shit out.

Katabasis

"The descent into Hell is easy"

—*Virgil, The Aeneid*

The Desires of Martyrdom

I.

The architect of your broken mind
has enjoyed transforming you into a cicada husk.
You wonder if anyone—anything can fill you now.
Can you ever be put back together?

II.

They say your papa admired
how your ~~man~~ humiliated you,
made you seek permission to exist.

He never questioned
how your starvation became so easy.

They say your mama knew:
that your place was at ~~his~~ feet
—you needed to be ~~his~~ chosen one,
~~his~~ sacred vessel.

Do they protect you now? Are they keeping vigil
by your bedside?

III.

You know there's no hero,
and you may be a damsel,
but these days no one wants
to rescue you (anymore).

The world remains heavy.
You gave all of yourself without questioning
where the pieces of you went.

May 22nd, 2017: She sits on my throat and makes it hard to talk

Remixed poem from Allison Mack's Blog

I.

A part of me rages raw—

the other has become the most intrusive
and obnoxious monster—
a hatchling of the Night Hag.

She wears essential oils like armor,
preaches about yoga, in her messy bun
and decorative athleisure wear.
She wants everyone to be envious
of how healthy *She* appears.
She is an enlightened soul
obsessed with interdependence
(watch her aura glow).

II.

I have become a pinched, pre-programmed robot
rehearsed in the practice of asking for permission.
Just five minutes—I am starting new; enough time to

let the pressure lift.

June 13th, 2017: She's cramped in a closet
Remixed poem from Allison Mack's Blog

Hummingbird heartbeat,
I quiver, as I peek through the closet door.

I hide from the world.
In the dark I am:
Raw.
My cellulite jiggles.
I am imperfect, disgustingly flawed.
The part of me that bleeds
is a voyeur.

I send out my representative, the "Allison-bot,"
and she never has armpit stains.
She is the grande dame—sassy with a hand
on her hip; flirty with a wink,
always has a clever retort.

I feel myself outgrowing this hiding spot—
I want to jump out from behind the door.
...Maybe tomorrow.

Sister/Traitor

At one time they might've called you sister.
You seemed the type they could get tangled
in conversations with, share tea and a dosa;
they'd shuffle tarot cards for you.
You were a person they could wander
the streets of London with, huddle together
to share a secret on the Tube before running
into the night filled with neon.

You were the kind to bury your feet in the hot sand
of Oahu, eating Thai food on the beach, drinking cold water
from delicately carved tin cups as condensation dripped
through your fingers. After dinner they'd place
a plumeria blossom in the palm of your hand,
because you'd try your best not to crush it.

But you've sold them out for a ~~man~~ who speaks
in keyrings, doesn't want a woman who can spit flames,
(or who looks like a grown woman). You helped keep
them on the edge of exhaustion, famished—hollow.
You promised a safe-home of sisterhood,
but burned their flesh all for ~~his~~ glory,
Because it makes ~~him~~ need you,
Because you think only ~~he~~ can give you
A purpose.
You are
                                    the deserter.

**June 11th, 2017: She tries to be good, and she failed
again...at least this time it was better**
Remixed poem from Allison Mack's Website

I see all the faces on the Tube—
we are all little 4 and 5 year olds
striving to be good—wanting
the gold-star, the pat on the head;
let us be acknowledged in some way.

I'm in pain from constantly smiling.
The façade that we are constructed to be
objects of perfection.

Sometimes, I feel like a knot
of muscle and nerves
that cannot be untied.

My struggle isn't special;
I too want a lollipop,
a promise *I will be ok.*

Allison, wake up! June 24th, 2017
Remixed poem from <u>*Frank Report*</u>

Push back.

There's a sickness over your head—
a box you placed yourself in.

You're a scared little girl,
wanting to be loved by everyone—
once peach-tea sweet,
but ~~he~~ has   torn   and   twisted you
into anathema.   You are a victim
of ~~his~~   treacherous mind games,   lost.

I know you; you want to crumble—
cannot handle knowing people
want you to burn, but you,
you are sprinting into an abyss

for a ~~man~~ who thinks   you are as   inconsequential
as a nickel.
~~he~~   will let you rot away in a cell,
let you crawl through broken glass
and die   for ~~him~~—as long as it's for ~~him~~

You've wanted to leave before—
listen to your gut, get out. *Run.*

What you invited into your home

I hope it haunted you. Your gilded
furniture may have looked beautiful.
You might've decorated with flowers and tapestries,
lit candles to make it sweet and cozy—
but we know what torments this place held—
what ghosts you created here.

We have heard from the survivors.
Maybe their sobs and screams invaded
your sleep—nights after the branding.
You were just following orders—
but ~~he~~ doesn't have to live with
poltergeists rattling ~~his~~ walls.

Toady demons can't see or hear spirits—
Not until they're banished to hell
where cacodemons belong.

June 24th, 2017: She heard them whisper
Remixed poem from Allison Mack's Website

The leaves have not yet fallen,
but they were talking.
the whole street was whispering my secrets.

The color you remember being

was vibrant and rich—
the inside of an ember,
saturated like the bright sandstone
earth of Sedona after
a long awaited rain.

The shocking smoothness
of the mercurochrome
you would pour on your belly
when infection set in a week after piercing.

You wanted to grow into a blood orange—
contain the sunniness of the rind,
and the dark crimson flesh that seemed
deep enough to drown in.

And here you are:
a faded watercolor gray,
like after an artist uses droplets
to lift the paint—erase a mistake.

July 1st, 2017: And she felt the comfort of another heartbeat in the house...
Remixed poem from Allison Mack's Website

I sit next to you—wherever you are.
I feel the heartbeat of the stories and myths
I *create* for you.

July 5th, 2017: She doesn't know if she's outside or inside out

Remixed poem from Allison Mack's Website

My life's study—the quest to find myself,
has led to identity suicide—I have been broken,
the yolk of me running in different directions.

I may never find the spine of *myself,*
I depend on things outside of me
to determine who I am and how I feel.
The films I watch, the different songs I listen to—
I morph into the most powerful people around me:
mimic the cadence in voices, think of the shirt
they'd wear and buy copies, hold my drink
the way I saw them do it once,
learn to fall in step with them.

I'm a little girl dying to be what she sees as most heroic;
it's hard to imagine that there is another option.

If you wanted to be saved

I.

The ~~man~~ you'd latched onto
should've been a drifter
in a dust storm you   wandered
through when
          lost.

You were so lonely,
~~he~~ had all the right words
tucked into ~~his~~ pocket;
~~he~~ told you about the constellations
~~he~~ saw rising in your eyes
(*and yes, they were really there,*
but the stars are so   faded   these days,
the night sky might not call
them back).

II.

At the pink theater in Mexico
you were still hoping to find   yourself.

You spent years sacrificing pieces of   your mind
          and
flesh
for a ~~man~~   you thought was
  (~~wanted to be~~)   God.

~~he~~ has made you: a marionette—tethered
                    a husk—missing days when you felt
filled.

III.

True Gods died here, in this little lush town,
centuries before your toes touched the ground.

They still hear you confess:
Your sins etched on your bones.
Part of you is always longing for home.

Astray

"I chose to disclose that Allison Mack attempted to recruit me into her 'women's circle' as I felt it was my responsibility to speak up...I didn't sign up to be an apologist for her or that vile cult. She struck me as a haunted, lost soul and that's the truth." -Samia Shoaib

Push your plate to the side
because ~~he~~ wants your bones
to be what ~~he~~ feels, and ~~he~~
wants your brains a mess
to play with.

People say you're a ghost these days,
or demon waiting in the shadows.
Maybe you're a puzzle that needs
to be put together—you'll always
feel you have pieces missing.

Path one: a·me·lio·rate

"The day misspent,
the love misplaced,
has inside it
the seed of redemption.
Nothing is exempt
from resurrection."

—<u>Kay Ryan, Say Uncle</u>

Nourishment
Remixed poem from Allison Mack's Website

I am the barren wasteland of boredom
—a desert in the middle of summer.
There is no relief from this drought.

I long for the days spent driving
through traffic on Laurel Canyon,
writing poetry in coffee shops,
seeing movies—(fingertips butter coated
from the popcorn) in old fashioned
movie theaters with velvet seats.
I pine for nights spent in art galleries,
drinking white wine and nibbling
on brie and olive oil soaked crostini.

I crave our Soul Food Sunday nights:
filled with twinkle lights, readings, writing,
feasting on decadent desserts:
pastries dusted with powdered sugar
—filled with pink strawberry cream.
It was our magic hour—
we filled one another up.

I was nourished.

July 8th: She started to recognize stories of redemption
Remixed poem from Allison Mack's Website

Insurmountable and disturbing,
I have fallen victim to ~~him~~   (and my own
impotence).

One day I'll wake up ready to mold my own life—
to heal and redeem what was left of my soul.

July 15th: She and herself had a nice long day together
Remixed poem from Allison Mack's Website

     I.

I put myself in hot water.
I traveled alone—got lost in a thick fog.
I scarred myself with pigment and indentations
as a way to disprove my own value,
but puncture wounds were an attention strategy.
I found approval in the ~~man~~   next to me.

     II.

I walked along the cobblestone streets of the North East.
I danced along the Los Angeles coastline.
I saw a curandera in the Southwest—
she gave me Yerba Buena tea,
(told me I needed to find where I left the real me).
 I watched the smoky sunset, as the wind rushed
over my body. And for the first time, in a decade
I interacted with my "self."

She was my long lost friend.

Path Two: The Devil, Hanged Man, and the 8 of Swords

"And this is the forbidden truth, the unspeakable taboo - that evil is not always repellent but frequently attractive; that it has the power to make of us not simply victims, as nature and accident do, but active accomplices."

—*Joyce Carol Oates*

Bound and Blindfolded

Deep in the fen, they came prepared to cut away at the rope,
undo the knots of the cloth covering your face
to lead you out of the spatha cage you made,
the door was already open.

When they came near, you raged—
sliced your skin, tributaries of blood,
staining the marshland you trapped yourself in.
Even then they tried to call you out
into a vast blooming meadow.

You are the sacrifice, the victim—
and maybe your ~~god~~ will rescue you
if you prove you are a worthy maiden.
After all, ~~he~~ helped you build this:
handed the swords to you one by one,
placed ~~his~~ palms over yours
and pressed the metal into the sand.
~~he~~ convinced you that staying in this prison
was your destiny.

If you open your eyes, you'll find
you can slip through without carving
your flesh too deep.

pittura infamante

~~his~~ cock didn't make you a better woman,
not like ~~he~~ promised,

but you're still willing to throw away
whatever is left of your life
for this roach of a ~~man~~.

~~he~~ kissed you, and you were a pawn,
a pied piper leading pretty young girls
to ~~his~~ home—~~his~~ California king-sized bed.

~~he~~ took you apart and said it would help you grow,
sewed ~~his~~ belief system into your heart—
now it demolishes you from within.

~~he~~ dickmatized you into signing an eternal vow
to be only ~~his~~, and groom the others to ~~his~~ liking,
told you ~~his~~ cum would save them in Armageddon.

You are the infinite fool,
~~he~~ holds no charisma for the rest of us.

the Luciferian

I.

~~he~~'s still the devil you've tethered yourself to.
~~he~~ consumed the flesh you offered ~~him~~—
sucked the skin and meat from your bones,
and yet ~~he~~ commands—desires more.

Give it all away for ~~him~~:
tattered dignity, and sanity.
Let deliverance evaporate
into the ether. Hunker down—
it's easier to stay in the world ~~he~~
convinced you was real.

Drink some more of ~~his~~ arsenic-laced words,
swallow them with a nice red wine, or milk
they'll keep you ensnared and safe
in this reverie.

II.

There were some who hoped
you might awaken from the nightmare
you slowly constructed over the years.
The demon that rooted itself in you,
would spew out from your mouth like an inky bile.

You'd be healed and saved—worthy of your beauty.
Everyone loves a redemption arc. They want the pretty,
pale girl to renounce sin, to admit the monster
lured her, hypnotized her, promised daily paradise.

You were under a spell no one could resist.

Limbo

"One can never truly leave. And never quite return. Do you understand?"

—*Emma Richler, Be My Wolff*

Are you awake now, Allison?

Or are you still slumbering away
under a bed of leaves, dreaming of Albany?

Tell us, you've started sanitizing the sleep
from your eyes—have wandered through
the forest of nightmares you created
under the command of an impotent ~~master.~~

Show us, you see the tapeworm
~~he~~ is. We know ~~he~~ fed on you,
made you weak and dizzy—how ~~he~~
grew, bloated as ~~he~~ drained
the nutrients from your body
during your twenties and thirties

Prove you removed ~~him~~ from your being—
have swallowed the medicine, went under
the knife—so every bit is gone and no
new toxicity can hatch.

Prospect

They are asking for your head. They don't want you in their
living rooms discussing books, and gender politics.

They don't want to share what haunts them,
how they try to heal in the light and darkness.

You are marked with more than just a branding iron.

Woman

"I spent so much time throughout my life listening to music about being 'beautiful without doing anything,' being 'an independent woman, being every woman...the 'fierce' and phenomenal woman' lie is so encouraged and pervasive. It is the root of such pride, such violence, such prejudice."
 -Allison Mack in an email to ~~keith raniere~~

I wonder who will trust you now.

I pity you. The times I have lost myself,
I knew in my bones, I must find
my own way back—no man
could save me, lead me down
a path. I must make my own magic.

But you swallowed the propaganda
of a foul ~~man~~, whose hatred of us
was so deep in ~~his~~ gut—~~he~~ made
a game of trying to break women—
grinding them into bone dust.

~~he~~ doesn't know the power
we can harness—we can bloom
with rebirth, capture starlight
just before it fades at dawn—
destroy with floods of rage.
We are feral—not meant to be
tamed by pitiful men.

~~his~~ idea of beauty is microscopic—
and you shrunk yourself to fit it.

How do you come back to yourself
from this? How do you mend
the parts you demolished in yourself—
is this the woman you always wanted to be?

Lessons

For years, you relieved yourself of the burden
of being a formidable woman, of finding your own
potential and power. Pam was a false prophet too,
she saw how pliable you were—she could mold
you into her own image, a new *wife* for a monster.
The falsifiers and grifters helped you construct
an imaginary world, then burned it down with their
greed and selfish lusts (that were forced onto others).

And if you come seeking forgiveness now,
not all of us will offer it. Many will turn you away—
the betrayer. Some will see themselves in you,
know what it's like to seek validation from
some unworthy being, and they can help
you find the tools to heal yourself.

Come humbled. Listen. Watch how sisters
can truly be bonded without scorching the Earth,
and each other. Learn what it's like to not have
a ~~man~~ at the root of everything you do—
the connection to everyone you know.

A final reminder

"Well, I'm trying to break her," ~~keith raniere~~ *discussing Allison Mack with Mark Vicente*

This is what ~~he~~ wanted—
you in pieces, completely
vulnerable—the perfect puppet.

Don't give ~~him~~ anymore.
Cut the soul strings—
do spells to cleanse your pussy,
heart, and mind of ~~his~~ bullshit.

Put yourself together—
become a whole ecosystem
pulsating with life.

Notes On Previous Publications

Expecting adoration was first published in Poetry WTF?!, May 2018

July 3rd, 2014: Collecting Heroes was first published in Anti-Heroin Chic, June 2018
Allison, Wake up! June 24, 2017 was first published in Anti-Heroin Chic, June 2018
An Accomplice: November 23rd, 2017 was first published in Anti-Heroin Chic, June 2018

November 5th, 2014: You know those days… was first published in Mojave He[art] Review, July 2018; subsequently published in Pink Plastic House, October 2020

The color you remember being was first published in Spider Mirror, August 2018; subsequently published in Pink Plastic House, April 2021

Sister/Traitor was first published in God is in the TV: Poetry Spotlight, October 2018

Je ne sais quoi was first published in Midnight Lane Boutique, October 2018
Love-bombed: November 23rd, 2017 was first published in Midnight Lane Boutique, October 2018
March 14th, 2014: My Global Museum Tour, Museum #2: The Neue Galerie was first published in Midnight Lane Boutique, October 2018

Elements of you was first published in Manzano Mountain Review, November 2018

Bound and Blindfolded was first published in Feminine Collective, December 2018

December 16th, 2011: 7 Stages was first published in
IceFloe Press, June 2020

The Introduction: November 14, 2006 was first published in
Burning House Press, October 2020

The Luciferian was first published in ArLiJo, May 2022

What you invited into your home was first published in
ArLiJo, May 2022

Acknowledgements

First and foremost I want to thank my parents, and my sisters, Beth and Becca for their unwavering support. My Aunt Eleanor for always believing in me.

For Eric who encouraged me as I wrote and edited. Thank you Tami, Lynne, Selena, and Sarah C. for reading my work. For Cindal who sat with me as I did additional research. For April, and Emma who showed me the importance of celebrating the little moments and big wins.

Thank you, Sera for seeing my potential and starting me on my writing journey back in 2003. You have inspired me in so many ways. Thank you Kendall B. for showing me that I could create collections, and share them with the world.

Athena, you have been with me since the beginning of this project. Thank you for reading each and every version of my poems, and offering thoughtful and constructive feedback. Thank you for the writing sessions, for the various Skype calls where we brainstormed. Thank you for pushing me to keep sending this manuscript out, even when I wanted to give up. I appreciate your friendship in so many ways.

Much gratitude to Emily and Savannah for understanding my work and helping me share it with the world. It has been a joy working with you.